CATASTROPHE!

EARTHQUAKE
DISASTERS

John Hawkins

FRANKLIN WATTS
LONDON•SYDNEY

First published in 2012 by Franklin Watts

Copyright © 2012 Arcturus Publishing Limited

Franklin Watts
338 Euston Road
London NW1 3BH

Franklin Watts Australia
Level 17/207 Kent Street, Sydney NSW 2000

Produced by Arcturus Publishing Limited,
26/27 Bickels Yard, 151–153 Bermondsey Street, London SE1 3HA

Text: John Hawkins
Editors: Joe Harris and Penny Worms
Design: Graham Rich
Cover design: Graham Rich

Picture credits:
Corbis: cover, 13, 14b, 15, 19, 20b, 30b, 32, 42, 44. Getty: 1, 16, 22b, 24, 28, 29, 35, 38, 39, 40, 44 (all except top), 45 (all), 47. Rex Features: 5, 37, 41. Science Photo Library: 4, 6, 7, 8, 9, 10, 13. Shutterstock: 12, 14t, 16, 18, 20t, 22t, 25, 26, 27, 30t, 34, 36, 40.

Cover image: Otsuchi village, Iwate prefecture, Japan. Villagers clamber over sheets of twisted metal in the wake of the Japanese earthquake and tsunami, 14 March 2011.

A CIP catalogue record for this book is available from the British Library.

Dewey Decimal Classification Number 363.3'495

ISBN 978 1 4451 1016 5

Printed in China

Franklin Watts is a division of Hachette Children's Books, an Hachette UK company.
www.hachette.co.uk

SL001926EN
Supplier 03, Date 0112, Print Run 1424

Contents

What Is an Earthquake?

Earthquakes are the result of movements in the earth's crust, which is the hard, rocky top layer on which we live. These movements cause the ground to shake, sometimes very violently. They can bring buildings crashing to the ground and twist or break up roads, railway lines and bridges. A major quake that hits a densely populated area can kill hundreds of thousands of people.

RIPPLING GROUND

An earthquake actually happens some way beneath the surface of the earth, at a point called the focus. The place on the surface of the earth above the focus is the epicentre. Shock waves from an earthquake can travel a long way, spreading through the ground like ripples spread through water.

Each year the earth experiences more than 50,000 earthquakes, although most of these are so small they are only detected by sensitive measuring instruments.

REVENGE OF THE GODS

Earthquakes have happened ever since the earth formed a solid surface 3.8 billion years ago. People long ago did not know what caused earthquakes and often made up legends about them, or believed their gods were responsible for the terrifying events.

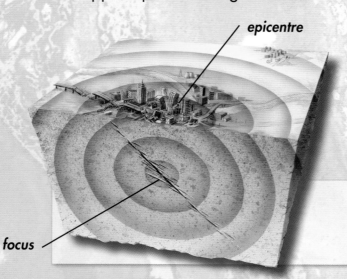

epicentre

focus

Shock waves ripple out from the focus of an earthquake. Above ground, they travel over the surface from the epicentre.

A devastating earthquake struck Mexico City in 1985. Around 30,000 people are thought to have died.

DANGER AREA

Earthquakes are most dangerous for people when they strike built-up areas. There is less danger for people living in the countryside but an earthquake can trigger other hazards such as landslides, floods and avalanches.

EARTHQUAKE AT SEA

Even if the epicentre of an earthquake is out at sea, the ripples of seismic waves can travel far inland and may still be strong enough to topple buildings. Earthquakes under the sea often cause tsunamis, massive waves that flood huge areas of land. Tsunamis are frequently responsible for more deaths than falling buildings when an earthquake happens beneath or near the sea.

Moving Lands

If the surface of the earth were a single piece, like the skin of an orange, we probably wouldn't have any earthquakes. But it is actually several pieces fitted together like a jigsaw puzzle – more like an orange skin that has been peeled off and then pieced back together.

TECTONIC PLATES

The earth's crust is broken up into chunks that fit together to cover the whole surface of the earth. These chunks are called tectonic plates. There are seven large plates and many smaller ones. Beneath the crust is slow-moving, semi-molten hot rock, nearly 3,200 km (about 2,000 miles) deep.

EARTH AND SEA

Six of the large tectonic plates carry land or a mix of land and sea, but much of the Pacific Ocean is on a single, vast plate of its own. Land-bearing crust is thicker and older than ocean-bearing crust. It is also lighter, so it floats higher on the semi-molten rock underneath. The tectonic plates are slowly moving all the time – at about the speed your fingernails grow – and some travel more quickly than others. Although they move very slowly, their movement is relentless.

250 million years ago, all the land on earth was clustered into a single, huge continent.

CONTINENTAL DRIFT

As the plates move, the continents gradually shift around the globe. The Atlantic Ocean is actually growing wider, so North America and Europe are moving away from each other.

inner core

outer core

lower mantle

upper mantle

The crust makes up less than one per cent of the earth's thickness. The layer of very hot rock underneath is called the mantle. The very top part of the upper mantle and the crust together make up the tectonic plates.

ONE CONTINENT

Around 250 million years ago, all the landmasses on earth were grouped together in a single vast continent called Pangea (meaning 'all land'). Before Pangea, there had been other arrangements of the land. Over millions of years, the landmasses have moved and broken up to reshape the continents completely.

Why Earthquakes Happen

The lines where tectonic plates meet are called faults. Most earthquakes occur along faults. As the plates push or grind against each other, pressure builds up. The ground does not move smoothly, and tension builds up before the plates finally lurch into a new position. This lurch can be sudden, moving the plates several centimetres or more.

WAVE AFTER WAVE

Ripples of energy, called seismic waves, spread out from the focus of an earthquake in all directions. Different types of wave move in different ways and at different speeds.

BEFORE AND AFTER

Foreshocks are tremors (small earthquakes) that happen as the ground begins to shift just before a large earthquake begins. Aftershocks happen days or even months later, as the plates settle down.

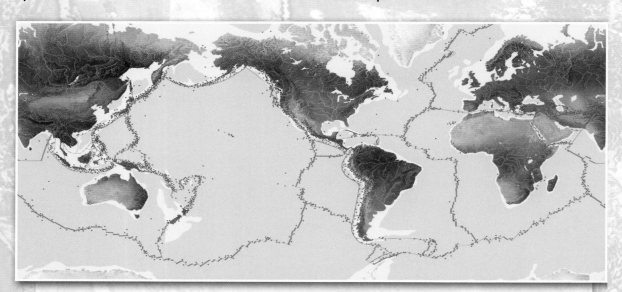

The grey lines on this map show the edges of the earth's tectonic plates. The red dots are the sites of major earthquakes.

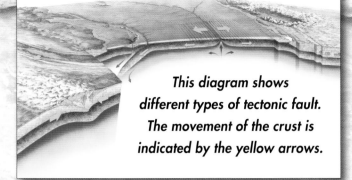

This diagram shows different types of tectonic fault. The movement of the crust is indicated by the yellow arrows.

TYPES OF FAULT

There are three types of fault. At a convergent (or destructive) fault, tectonic plates push into each other, forcing the land upward. The Himalayas were formed this way and they are still being forced upward at a rate of 5 cm (2 inches) per year, as India moves northward, pushing into Tibet.

At a divergent (or constructive) fault, plates move apart and new rock from the mantle comes up to the surface. This is happening in the middle of the Atlantic Ocean, where lava from under the ground forms new land. The Atlantic Ocean is growing by a few centimetres every year.

At a transform (or conservative) fault, plates grind against each other as they move in different directions. There is a transform fault in California, where one plate is moving north and one south.

THE RING OF FIRE

Because the Pacific Ocean is on a large tectonic plate of its own, there are borders with other plates all the way around the ocean. Most of the boundary of the Pacific plate is vulnerable to earthquakes. There are earthquakes on the US west coast, in parts of western South America, and around Japan, eastern China and eastern Russia. Some of these areas – Japan, eastern Russia and parts of Central and South America – also have many volcanoes. The rim of the Pacific is called the Ring of Fire because of these volcanoes.

Predicting Earthquakes

In the past, foreshocks were the only warning people had that an earthquake was about to happen. Today, seismologists (scientists who study earthquakes) are better informed and have special monitoring equipment, but some quakes give no warning.

This early seismograph was used to monitor ground movement in Italy near the volcano Mount Vesuvius.

WATCHING WAVES

A seismograph is an instrument that picks up movement of the ground. In a simple seismograph, a suspended pen draws a line on a piece of paper. A ground shake makes the line wobble, and large spikes in the line show significant tremors. Modern seismographs use computers that immediately carry out calculations from the recordings.

EPICENTRE

A single seismograph can only indicate the distance between the seismograph and the epicentre of a quake, so the epicentre could be anywhere: north, south, east or west. It takes information from three seismographs in different places to pinpoint the exact epicentre.

SPACE WATCH

Seismologists use information from satellites orbiting the earth to tell them when the ground is shifting or bulging, and an earthquake may be on the way. They also survey the land along fault lines.

MEASURING EARTHQUAKES

Seismologists have developed two different methods of measuring an earthquake's intensity and severity. The Richter scale applies a number between 1 and 10 to an earthquake depending on the amount of ground movement it causes. Quakes that register below 3 on the scale cannot be felt by people. A severe earthquake measures between 7 and 7.9, and a very severe earthquake measures over 8. No earthquake has measured over 9.5.

INTENSITY

The Modified Mercalli Intensity scale records levels of damage. The scale goes from I, Instrumental (detected only by scientific instruments) to XII, Catastrophic (with the ground moving in waves, and all structures destroyed).

 LEARNING FROM CATASTOPHES

It appears that animals react to an earthquake long before people can feel any tremors. In China and Japan, there are stories of snakes coming out of the ground, of dogs howling and even pandas holding their heads in their paws. Chinese scientists prompted the evacuation of the Chinese city of Haicheng in 1975 after observing unusual animal behaviour. Several hours later, a massive earthquake destroyed 90 per cent of the city.

Disaster Strikes Japan, 2011

The Japanese people are well prepared for earthquakes. They have experienced many, but none on the scale of the Tohoku Earthquake of 11 March 2011. It was the fifth most powerful earthquake in recorded history and it set off a catastrophic chain reaction.

WARNINGS

There had been strong foreshocks both days and just hours before. Japan's earthquake warning system raised the alarm and the Meteorological Agency issued a tsunami warning. Japan was poised.

THE BIG ONE

The major quake came at 2.46 pm with a magnitude of 9.0. It was the largest Japan had ever experienced. It occurred under the ocean, approximately 130 km (80 miles) off the northeast coast of Japan, at a depth of only 32 km (20 miles).

The violent tremors rocked buildings in Tokyo, a distant 370 km (230 miles) away. The damage was widespread but not disastrous. Worse was to come.

TSUNAMIS

As expected, the earthquake triggered tsunamis. The waves that hit the northeast coast were so powerful that they picked up cars and ships like bath toys, and smashed houses into each other. The waves travelled up to a staggering 10 km (6 miles) inland. The official death toll was 14,800 people dead with a further 10,000 missing.

A tsunami survivor weeps amid debris in the devastated town of Natori, in the worst hit area of the Tohoku region in northeast Japan.

NUCLEAR PANIC

Japan's nightmare was not over. The Fukushima nuclear plant went into automatic shutdown after the earthquake, but the tsunami caused the emergency generators to fail. A large explosion in one of the reactors caused a mass evacuation of the area. It was the second worst nuclear accident in history.

WHY DID IT HAPPEN?

Japan is in one of the most seismically active places in the world. It sits on an fault line where the Pacific tectonic plate is being forced under the Eurasian plate. In 2011, an extreme build-up of tension caused a major slippage, triggering the earthquake and tsunami. It also caused the level of Japan's coast to drop, so the waves travelled faster and further inland than expected.

HAITI

Collapse in Haiti, 2010

Haiti is an extremely poor country in the Caribbean. The Haitian people have suffered much, but the earthquake that struck on 12 January 2010 was truly devastating. It killed 316,000 people, one person in every fifteen living in the area.

COLLAPSE

The magnitude 7.0 earthquake occurred only 16 km (10 miles) from the densely populated capital of Port-au-Prince. Aftershocks continued to shake the badly constructed buildings. They simply collapsed and much of the city disintegrated into rubble. Over a million people lost their homes.

An injured Haitian girl sleeps with her mother and brother after being treated at an emergency clinic.

HELPLESS

Neighbours pulled the injured from rubble, but they could do little more. Much of the city's infrastructure was in ruins. Roads were blocked; hospitals had collapsed; the police force was decimated. Even part of the presidential palace had fallen down. Many officials were dead or injured.

A search-and-rescue team help a woman who had been trapped for five days.

AID ARRIVES

Haiti needed help and aid agencies were keen to provide it, but the scale of the destruction made their work harder. The airport and the road to Port-au-Prince had suffered damage. When rescue teams did arrive, they had trouble moving around. Medical teams were overstretched, in spite of aid money flooding in.

SLOW PROGRESS

Six months on, rubble was still everywhere and tarpaulins remained the only protection for the homeless. Some progress had been made. Schools had reopened and more people had access to fresh water and toilets than before the quake. However, rebuilding would take years, maybe even a generation.

EYEWITNESS

Carel Pedre, a TV and radio presenter in Port-au-Prince told the BBC: 'It's dark outside, there is no electricity, all the phone networks are down, so there's no way that people can get in touch with their family and friends. There are aftershocks every 15 to 20 minutes. I didn't see any emergency services.... People don't know where to go or where to start.'

SHENSI

China's Devastating Quakes

An earthquake that shook the Shensi (or Shaanxi) province of China on the night of 23 January 1556 is thought to be the worse natural disaster in recorded history in terms of lives lost. Estimated to be of a magnitude of 8.0 to 8.3 on the Richter scale, it devastated 98 counties and 8 provinces of Central China.

830,000 DEAD

The destruction spanned 1,300 sq km (500 square miles) and in some counties the average death toll was 60 per cent of the population. A total of 830,000 people lost their lives according to imperial records. This was because many lived in poorly constructed houses or in man-made caves dug into soft clay cliffs.

NIGHT TERROR

The earthquake also struck at night when most people were indoors, causing a higher death toll. Survivors of the initial quakes also found themselves victims of fires, landslides and floods caused, in part, by the quake. The tremor was so big that people felt it in over half of China.

Imperial Chinese records provide information on the number of casualties in the 1556 earthquake.

1920s DISASTER

Another earthquake of magnitude 8.6 on the Richter scale hit the Chinese province of Kansu to the northwest on 16 December 1920, killing some 180,000 people directly. A further 20,000 are thought to have died due to lack of shelter during the bitter winter that followed.

1950s QUAKE

An even more catastrophic earthquake is thought to have happened in the same area in the mid-1950s. Some estimates of the death toll put it even higher than the 1556 record holder. Up to a million people may have died, but no official details were released to the rest of the world.

A Turkish Tragedy, 526 CE

In the sixth century CE, Antioch (near Antakya in Turkey) was a big, bustling city, important to both the Roman Empire and the early Christian community. On 29 May 526 CE, the city was busier than usual. Thousands of Christians had flocked there for the feast of Ascension the next day. They couldn't have known what was about to happen.

THE INITIAL QUAKE

Soon after 6 pm, when people had gone indoors at dusk, the earthquake struck without warning. Whole buildings collapsed in an instant, crushing those inside. An eerie silence followed. Then came the aftershocks, followed by a fast-moving fire.

FEROCIOUS FLAMES

The flames blocked any route of escape. Survivors were burned to death as they fled. Those trapped under the rubble were suffocated by smoke or died in the flames. It is estimated that between 250,000 and 300,000 people were killed in the initial shock and fire, or perished later among the rubble.

THIEVES AND BANDITS

Hordes of thieves descended on the ruins, robbing the dead and tearing gold inlays and precious ornaments from the buildings. Bandits attacked survivors, stealing their valuables and murdering anyone who resisted.

Only ruins now remain of the Roman road to Antioch.

MYSTERIES AND MIRACLES

Tales of miracles circulated. Pregnant women trapped under the rubble emerged up to three weeks later with healthy babies. Other survivors said they saw a cross in the sky three days after the earthquake. They fell on their knees and gave thanks. However, no one could explain why God would cause such destruction.

EYEWITNESS

One of the few survivors, John Malalas, said that the 'fire fell down from heaven like rain…. Sparks of fire filled the air and burned like lightning. Except for the soil, the fire surrounded everything in the city, as if it had received a commandment from God that every living thing should be burned…. Not a single dwelling, nor house of any sort, no church, nor monastery, nor any other holy place was left intact.'

Mount St Helens Shakes, 1980

In 1980, a series of over 10,000 earthquakes shook Mount St Helens, a volcano not far inland from the Pacific coast of Washington State. The seismic activity under the earth was great enough to change the shape of the volcano. On 18 May, a large earthquake measuring 5.1 on the Richter scale caused a landslide, which in turn triggered a cataclysmic volcanic eruption.

A column of ash and gas rose more than 24 km (15 miles) into the atmosphere in only 15 minutes.

EXPLOSION

The landslide was the largest in recorded history. It released a huge build-up of pressure inside the volcano and triggered powerful explosions underneath the sliding debris. Rocks, gas, ash and steam blasted into the air at speeds of 480 kph (300 mph).

DESTRUCTION

A second eruption caused pyroclastic flows – avalanches of volcanic gas, dust and rocks. Snow melted to form dangerous lahars, flows of volcanic mud, that poured down the mountainside. The lahars flattened a vast area of trees. After the eruptions, Washington's fifth largest peak went from 2,950 m (9,677 feet) to 2,550 m (8,365 feet) and a large crater replaced the rounded summit.

HUMAN TOLL

The earthquakes themselves caused no loss of life, but the resulting eruptions devastated the forest area around Mount St Helens. Fortunately there were no towns within the paths of the pyroclastic flows and lahars, but still 57 people died. Millions of wild animals and salmon in local fisheries died.

WHY DID IT HAPPEN?

Mount St Helens is on the eastern side of the Ring of Fire, above a subduction zone, where the Juan de Fuca oceanic plate is pushing underneath the North American continental plate. A sudden surge in magma caused a build-up within the volcano and the side visibly bulged out. The earthquake caused the landslide which released the pressure, just as opening a can of soda releases bubbles from inside it. Even now, there are one or two small earthquakes in the region every day.

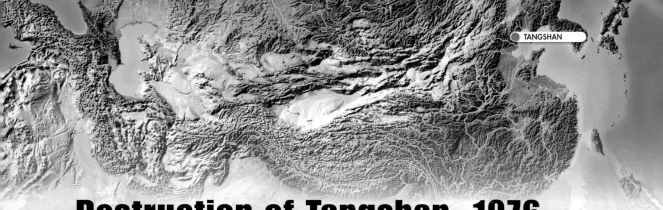

Destruction of Tangshan, 1976

Tangshan, a city of a million people, lies southeast of Beijing, in China. It is a centre for electricity generation. At 3.45 am on 29 July 1976, flashing lights, visible over 320 km (200 miles) away, appeared over the city. The heart of the city was completely destroyed in 23 seconds by an earthquake registering 7.8–8.2 on the Richter scale.

In just 23 seconds, the heart of the city of Tangshan was destroyed.

DESTRUCTION

Only the newer buildings survived. In some places, cracks several metres wide appeared in the earth. Fences were knocked out of line and railway tracks buckled. Thousands of sinkholes opened up, which looked like bomb craters.

SHOCK WAVES

Over 96 km (60 miles) away at Tientsin, the former prime minister of Australia Gough Whitlam and his wife fled from the seventh floor of their guest house, which they said 'literally split down the middle'. In Beijing, older structures collapsed. Six million people fled their homes and camped out in the torrential rainstorm that followed the initial shock of the earthquake.

RAPID RESCUE

By 5 pm, military planes were dropping food, water, medical supplies and clothing into the city.

The following day a huge number of aid workers and soldiers arrived from Beijing. They took the injured to hospitals and buried the dead quickly in mass graves outside the city to prevent an epidemic. Some 30,000 medical personnel, 30,000 construction workers and 100,000 troops were involved in the rescue operation.

 EYEWITNESS

Ho Shu-sen, a senior police officer, was woken by his wife moments before the earthquake hit. 'I saw a quick flash of greenish-blue light in the sky and heard a strange sound from under the ground. The floor began jerking up and down. I jumped out of the window, but the earth shook back and forth and threw me to the ground. My house collapsed. For two or three minutes there was no sound. Then I heard people crying everywhere in the darkness in the ruins of their homes.'

AFTERSHOCKS

In the next 48 hours, 125 aftershocks were recorded in north-east China. The strongest occurred 16 hours after the tremor that destroyed Tangshan. In all, it is estimated that 95 per cent of Tangshan's civil buildings and 80 per cent of its industrial plants suffered severe damage.

Aftermath: the city of Tangshan was reduced to rubble.

UNPREDICTED

The earthquake came as a shock to Chinese scientists, who previously had argued that they could predict earthquakes from the strange behaviour of animals and the sudden change in the level and temperature of water in wells. Indeed, just such a forecast in February 1975 had saved thousands of lives in Liaoning Province. But there was no warning at Tangshan.

HUGE DEATH TOLL

At first, the death toll was estimated at over 750,000. However, three years later, the Chinese authorities published the official figure as 242,000. A further 164,000 people were thought to be seriously injured and 2,600 children became orphans. The reason for the high death toll was that the epicentre was directly under the city and the earthquake happened at night, when most people were indoors.

REBUILDING

After some argument about whether they should rebuild on an earthquake-prone site, the city was rebuilt in 1979.

CHINESE BELIEFS

According to ancient Chinese beliefs, an earthquake is supposed to herald a major political upheaval, such as the end of a dynasty. Six weeks after the Tangshan earthquake, the Communist leader Mao Tse-tung died.

This monument shows former Chinese leader Mao Tse-tung.

MESSINA

'Messina is no more.' 1908

At 5.20 am on the rainy morning of 28 December 1908, the Sicilian port of Messina was rocked by the first of three earth tremors that destroyed 90 per cent of its buildings and killed the majority of its population of 100,000 in their sleep.

TSUNAMI

The epicentre of the earthquake, measuring 7.5 on the Richter scale, was under the Straits of Messina that separate the island of Sicily from the Italian mainland. Just as the survivors were emerging from the rubble, they were hit by an 8-m (26-foot) tsunami, which swept them out to sea. Others were burned to death when a ruptured gas main set the town on fire. Nobody is sure how many died.

DEATHTRAPS

Some families survived because they lived in small, well-built houses. The large houses of the rich were deathtraps. Messina's impressive palaces and public buildings had thin, high walls made of pebbles bound together with cheap cement, despite the city being severely damaged by an earthquake in 1783. The cement turned to dust at the first tremor. The cathedral, the army barracks, the military hospital and the hotels all fell down.

A few lucky survivors wander through the ruins of Messina.

 ## EYEWITNESS

Survivor, Rosina Calabresi, told a newspaper reporter simply: 'Messina non esiste più,' or 'Messina is no more.' She and her husband, along with their son Francesco, his wife, and their two children, managed to escape into the rain. 'The earth groaned as it rocked from side to side as if it were in pain,' said Francesco. 'Though the house fell down about us we were not hurt. The door to the street was jammed and would not open. I found a small hole in the wall near it and managed to crawl out through it and help the others out.'

SURVIVOR'S STORY

London shipbroker Constantine Doresa was staying at the Trinscria Hotel. After being jolted awake, he 'clutched at the sides of the bed, which seemed to be falling through space…. Then came a series of crashes, the roof falling around me. I was smothered in brick and plaster…. I felt for matches, struck a light and was horrified to find my bed on the side of an abyss.'

The rescue operation in Messina discovered very few people alive under the rubble.

RESCUE

With the aid of knotted sheets, Doresa and his travelling companion managed to lower themselves to safety, rescuing a Swedish couple on the way. They later returned to the hotel with the crew of a Welsh steamer, some Russian sailors, and ladders and ropes to rescue other guests. Eyewitness accounts tell of half-naked survivors stumbling injured through the rubble of the streets.

LOOTING BEGINS

Looters set about robbing the shops and warehouses, and stripping the corpses of their valuables. Even law-abiding survivors were forced to forage for food, water and clothing. Russian sailors who arrived in Messina first did what they could to prevent looting. British and Italian ships rushed to the port to help. Soon relief poured in from all over Italy, Europe and the United States.

DEATH TOLL

Estimates at the time put the death toll as high as 90,000 in Messina itself and 40,000 in the mainland port of Reggio di Calabria. Another 27,000 were thought to have died in the towns and villages along the straits. The official figure was 120,000.

LEARNING FROM CATASTROPHES

After the 1908 earthquake, new building regulations were brought in and Messina was rebuilt with wide streets and low, reinforced-concrete buildings. The cathedral and the Church of Annunziata dei Catalani were restored and the National Museum houses works of art saved from the earthquake.

The port of Messina today.

ARMENIA

Armenia in Crisis, 1988

At 11.41 am on 7 December 1988, an earthquake measuring 6.9 on the Richter scale hit Armenia, a densely populated republic of the former Soviet Union that lies along the border with Turkey. Four minutes later, it was rocked again by an aftershock of magnitude 5.8.

Homeless survivors sit around a fire near their collapsed apartment building and wait to hear of family members feared trapped in the rubble.

TOWNS OBLITERATED

The town of Spitak was virtually 'erased from the face of the earth', as one reporter put it. In nearby Kirovakan, a city of some 170,000 people, almost every building of any size had collapsed. High-rise apartment buildings built from prefabricated concrete slabs became instant tombs for their unsuspecting inhabitants.

BUILDINGS COLLAPSED

At Leninakan, 48 km (30 miles) to the west, the ceiling of a classroom at Elementary School Nine on Gorky Street collapsed onto the 50 children below, while some 250 people were trapped inside a computer centre. The walls of the ancient cathedral collapsed, although the dome was left intact, and the Armenian Seismic Institute was destroyed. In all, an area of some 10,000 sq km (4,000 square miles) was devastated.

CRIES FOR HELP

The muffled cries of survivors came filtering up through the debris. Others were not so lucky. As volunteers attempted to clear the rubble, rows of corpses were lined up along the streets for identification and burial, while survivors wrapped in coats and blankets tried to warm themselves by hastily made bonfires.

WHY DID IT HAPPEN?

This region is prone to earthquakes, because it is where the Arabian tectonic plate is slowly colliding with the Eurasian plate, pushing up the Caucasus Mountains in the north. Geologists have since found a long scarp 1.6 metres (5 feet) high and 8 km (5 miles) long southeast of Spitak. It appears that one side of the fault rode up over the other.

RESCUE EFFORTS HAMPERED

Bringing relief to the stricken cities was almost impossible. Armenia is a mountainous country. Roads were blocked by landslides and the train line was cut. As an airlift got underway, a fog closed in and two planes bringing help and supplies crashed, killing all on board.

People lost mothers, fathers, sisters, brothers and children in the earthquake.

HELP AT LAST

Eventually the Soviet Army arrived with 6,500 troops and heavy bulldozers. Twenty-five brigades of military doctors were brought in, while the inhabitants of Moscow lined up to donate blood, blankets and clothing.

AMERICAN HELP

For the first time since World War II, the Soviets accepted American aid. Eight US government transport planes flew in earth-moving equipment and relief supplies. These were followed by 12 more supplied by charities.

GLOBAL HELP

In all, 67 nations came to Armenia's aid. The British brought sensitive listening devices and fibre-optic probes to hunt for survivors. The French brought sniffer dogs. The Germans sent cranes. The Japanese gave money, while the Italians erected prefabricated homes.

RACE AGAINST TIME

The relief workers soon found themselves in a race against time. The temperature plummeted and the rubble was soaked with freezing rain. At Elementary School Nine, a volunteer had recovered 48 corpses – then, miraculously, found one child alive. A week after the earthquake, 20 more survivors were dug out of the wreckage of Leninakan, and one more was found in Spitak. But that was it. Some 15,000 victims had been rescued and 25,000 dead bodies were found. No one is sure how many died in all.

EYEWITNESS

In a film made a year later by aidarmenia.com to help Armenia victims, a couple, Ashot and Astrick, painfully tell of their loss of nine members of their family, including their two children.

'December 7th may have been last year, but to us it feels as if that horror was yesterday.... It's only now we realize how happily we lived... but all that lasted a short time. The earthquake of December 7th personally proved to me that all of that could, as in a fairytale, vanish without a trace, leaving you alone.'

GUATEMALA

Guatemala Landslides, 1976

Guatemala is located in a geologically unstable region of Central America. The small country has nine volcanoes, one of which is the most active in Central America, and also suffers from earthquakes.

DANGER ZONE

On the night of 8 April 1902, an earthquake lasting 30–40 seconds left 20,000 dead in Quetzaltenango, Guatemala's second largest city. The rumblings continued for decades. Pressure was building.

LANDSLIDES

Then on 4 February 1976, a quake reaching 7.5 on the Richter scale was felt from Costa Rica to Mexico City. An earth movement of 1.5 m (5 feet) had happened on the fault line that passes through Guatemala. Landslides buried villages. Some 22,778 people

died and some 80,000 were injured. The quake damaged roads, railway lines and bridges, making it almost impossible to get relief to the needy.

CAPITAL CATASTROPHE

In Guatemala City, the electricity was cut off to prevent fire, plunging the capital into darkness. Fearful of aftershocks, hospital staff moved patients outside. Many more arrived with fractured spines and pelvises. Their houses had fallen on them as they slept. In poor areas, slums at the edge of the city slid down ravines, 20 or 30 houses at a time.

LOOTING

Looting began and gunfire was heard. A radio station warned of 'false medical helpers' who were giving injured victims an injection of morphine, then robbing them while they were unconscious.

AT FAULT

The fault line could be traced for 240 km (150 miles) with some cracks 10 m (33 feet) long and 10 cm (4 inches) wide. One native Guatemalan summed it up: 'You go to sleep and wake, and the world has changed.'

58,000 houses were destroyed in Guatemala City.

EYEWITNESS

18-year-old survivor Alfonso Amaya Montes heard his sister call, then found himself buried under a pile of rubble. Choking with dust, he had just enough breath to call out. An hour later, a man dug Alfonso out. His parents and sister were dead. 'I lost 11 relatives,' he said. 'They were buried without coffins, wrapped only in sheets. We could not have funerals. There were too many dead.'

San Francisco in Flames, 1906

The quake of 1906 earned San Francisco the name of 'Earthquake City'. This was not because there was a great loss of life – although there were an estimated 2,000 casualties – but because the United States had never experienced an earthquake on this scale before.

PRECARIOUS POSITION

San Francisco is close to two faults – the San Andreas fault, which runs up the coast of California, and the Hayward fault, which runs up the east side of the bay.

BUSTLING METROPOLIS

In 1906, San Francisco was a young city that had quickly become a financial, commercial and cultural centre. In terms of trade, it was second only to New York.

MASSIVE QUAKE

At 5.12 am on 18 April a massive earthquake, estimated at 8.2 on the Richter scale, struck the city. The first tremor lasted 40 seconds. A second lasted over a minute.

THE AFTERMATH

Wood-framed houses splintered. Pipes twisted. Fissures opened in the streets. Electrical wires gave off showers of blue sparks. Water mains burst and gas rose out of cracks in the street. Then came fire.

INFERNO

Within half an hour of the quake, more than 50 fires had started. These separate fires merged into one inferno. By early evening the fires had spread. The flames were so intense that steel beams melted. San Francisco's respected fire service had lost its chief in the quake, so the army took over. President Theodore Roosevelt ordered the mobilization of 2,000 troops to prevent looting, but there was little trouble that first night.

The San Andreas fault in California is clearly visible from the air.

 EYEWITNESS

The chief of the Postal Telegraph Cable Company sent out the first news of the earthquake at 6 am. The message he sent read: 'THERE WAS AN EARTHQUAKE AT FIVE FIFTEEN THIS MORNING, WRECKING SEVERAL BUILDINGS AND WRECKING OUR OFFICES. THEY ARE CARTING DEAD FROM THE FALLEN BUILDINGS. FIRE ALL OVER TOWN. THERE IS NO WATER AND WE HAVE LOST OUR POWER. I'M GOING TO GET OUT OF THE OFFICE AS WE HAVE HAD A LITTLE SHAKE EVERY FEW MINUTES.'

ESCAPE

Throughout the night, tens of thousands of stunned people fled the city. They watched from afar as the flames spread. Others left the city by train and boat.

After the quake many buildings had to be pulled down to make them safe.

ARMY EFFORT

The army battled the flames, trying to create firebreaks. They even resorted to gunpowder and shelling, but nothing worked. They created tent cities overnight for some 300,000 homeless people, and prisoners were sent to work digging latrines and graves.

THE NEXT DAY

By the afternoon of 19 April, the whole city east of Van Ness Avenue was on fire. The avenue was the widest in the city, so with artillery, kerosene and dynamite, the army demolished the buildings on the west side to make a fire-break 16 city blocks long. Just as the flames arrived, the wind changed. The western part of the city had been saved.

REBUILDING

In all, 28,188 buildings were destroyed. Crews had to work 24 hours a day, seven days a week, clearing the rubble. Businesses reopened within a week. Within two months, over 8,000 large wooden huts – each housing six to eight families – had been erected. The breadlines ended on 1 August, and by the following spring the rubble had gone. By 1909, construction workers paid three times the going rate had built 20,000 new houses.

LEARNING FROM CATASTROPHES

The city was rebuilt after the 1906 earthquake on the same layout as before, but the city planners now included a system of reservoirs, secondary water mains and cisterns to fight any future fire.

Whole streets collapsed as a result of the quake.

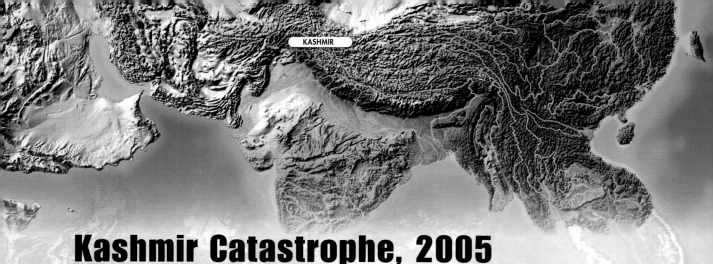

Kashmir Catastrophe, 2005

Kashmir is a mountainous region west of the Himalayas, between India and Pakistan. Before 8 October 2005, the greatest threat to its people was the open hostility between the Indian and Pakistani governments. However, it was an earthquake that sparked a real catastrophe.

RELENTLESS

The area is on a known fault line where relentless underground forces are pushing India into Asia. The quake was not huge, measuring about 7.6 on the Richter scale, but it happened closer to the earth's crust than usual. The neighbouring countries of Afghanistan, Tajikistan and China also felt the tremors, which began as Kashmiri students sat at their desks. Entire classes were wiped out in a few seconds.

DEATH TOLL

It took weeks to assess the death toll, but official figures released within a month of the disaster put it at about 75,000. Many more were injured.

AFTERSHOCKS

The quake fractured roads, and people travelling along tracks and footpaths were at risk from the landslides caused by the many aftershocks. Injured people waited in agony for evacuation by helicopter.

People pray in the ruins of a mosque in Balakot, Pakistan.

BACK TO BASICS

The Pakistani army had only 19 helicopters at its disposal. When international helicopters arrived, the crews could only watch as the vital supplies they dropped often bounced down the mountainsides into ravines, out of reach of the survivors. Trucks clogged up the only open roads so mules provided the most reliable mode of transport. Relief was painfully slow in arriving.

COOPERATION

Seasonal rains made rescue efforts difficult. With winter coming on, old enemies India and Pakistan opened up the disputed border in five places to allow refugees to cross.

HOMELESS

By the end of 2005, the United Nations estimated that 3 million Kashmiri people were still homeless. Five years later, some were still awaiting help to rebuild their lives.

 EYEWITNESS

When bulldozers finally opened remote roads, people came down from the hills to seek food and tents. Aleem Usmani started a 21-km (13-mile) walk to the regional capital Muzaffarabad. Returning home carrying 10 kg (22 lb) of flour and a bag full of supplies, he told a reporter, 'When you are hungry enough, you can carry it. No aid has come to my village.' He then resumed his long uphill trek home.

Looking to the Future

Although tectonic plates move, faults do not. The San Andreas fault will always run through San Francisco, and Japan will always be on the junction of three plates. For this reason, the places prone to earthquakes will always be in danger.

PREDICTION

Some faults are more active than others. Frequent small quakes occur where the plates move easily. Large quakes occur where stress builds up and the plate movement is sudden and severe. By studying the intervals between past earthquakes and measuring plate movements, seismologists are able to say which places may be due for a large earthquake, but they cannot say when. The people of San Francisco, for example, know they can expect a major earthquake in the next 20 years.

Children in Tokyo, Japan, shelter beneath a table during an earthquake drill. The practice will help them do the right thing if an earthquake strikes.

RICHTER SCALE RATING	HOW OFTEN?
0.5–2.0	8,000 per day
5	800 per year
7	18 per year
9	1 in 20 years

This table shows the approximate frequency of earthquakes, according to their size.

EVACUATION AND WARNING

In places where earthquakes are frequent, such as Japan, people practise earthquake drills so that they know what to do and where to go when the tremors start.

MORE OF THE SAME?

Even with the knowledge that a large earthquake will strike again in the future, people often want to carry on living in the same place. It is also difficult to balance people's desire for traditional homes with measures to make buildings safer. Safe buildings are more expensive to build and some communities are unable to afford them. Architects and engineers have devised methods to make buildings safer against earthquakes.

BUILDING SAFETY

Most methods work by allowing some movement in the building, so if an earthquake strikes the building can shake without falling down. In Japan, some structures hang from a central column that is firmly rooted in the ground, but the walls can move. Other buildings have rockers or shock absorbers built into their foundations.

EXTRAORDINARY POWER

Earthquakes can unleash a massive amount of power – the equivalent to around 1,000 nuclear bombs in the largest quakes. We will never be able to control or prevent them. However, we can try to predict them, and make preparations to minimize the tragic loss of life.

Timeline

29 May CE 526, Antioch, Turkey
Important to both Romans and Christians, the city of Antioch was destroyed by an earthquake and subsequent fire. The city never recovered.

23 January 1556, Shensi, China
The earthquake that hit this region in the 16th century is thought to be the worst natural disaster in recorded history in terms of lives lost. A total of 830,000 people died.

8 April 1902, Guatemala
An earthquake lasting 30–40 seconds left 20,000 dead in Quetzaltenango.

18 April 1906, San Francisco, USA
A big earthquake of 8.2 magnitude struck the city, followed by a long aftershock. Fires sprung up everywhere, building into an inferno that raged across the city.

28 December 1908, Messina, Italy
An earthquake of 7.5 magnitude shook the town of Messina in Sicily. A tsunami followed, sweeping away survivors. The official death toll was 120,000.

16 December 1920, Kansu, China
An earthquake of 8.6 magnitude hit this region in northwest China, killing some 180,000 people. A further 20,000 died in the harsh winter that followed.

Mid-1950s, Kansu, China
Not much is known about this earthquake, but it is thought that up to a million people may have perished.

4 February 1976, Guatemala

An earthquake measuring 7.5 was felt from Costa Rica to Mexico City. Landslides buried villages and Guatemala City was badly hit.

29 July 1976, Tangshan, China

It took just 23 seconds to flatten the city of Tangshan. This earthquake of 7.8–8.2 magnitude killed 242,000 people according to official figures, but unofficial estimates are far greater.

18 May 1980, Mount St Helens, USA

The volcano of Mount St Helens erupted dramatically after a long series of earthquakes caused a landslide on one of its flanks. There was widespread devastation and 57 people died.

7 December 1988, Armenia

An earthquake of magnitude 6.9 and subsequent aftershock shook a huge area and devastated the towns of Spitak and Kirovakan.

8 October 2005, Kashmir

Remote mountain villages were rocked by an earthquake measuring 7.6. Access was severely restricted, making rescue attempts slow and difficult. It is thought 75,000 people died.

12 January 2010, Haiti

Around Port-au-Prince, over a million people were made homeless and 316,000 killed, following an earthquake of magnitude 7.0.

11 March 2011, Japan

A massive offshore earthquake, magnitude 9.0, caused a catastrophic tsunami that killed up to 25,000 people. It triggered the second worst nuclear disaster in history.

Glossary

aftershock the shaking of the ground as it settles down after an earthquake

breadline a line of people waiting to receive free or rationed food given out by charities or official agencies

core the very hot centre of the earth, made of molten and solid metal

crust the hard, rocky surface of the earth

evacuate to move people out of an area to somewhere safer

fibre-optic probes long, thin, wire-shaped devices that have cameras at one end. Rescuers can thread them through small gaps in rubble to search for suvivors.

firebreak a strip of land that has been cleared to stop the spread of fire

foreshock the shaking of the ground that comes before the main movement of an earthquake

infrastructure large-scale public structures such as power and water supplies, public transportation, communications, roads and schools

kerosene a by-product of crude oil, kerosene is a type of fuel, used for heating and to run some small engines

lahar a deadly, often fast-moving mudlflow made up of volcanic material and water

lava molten rock that comes from within the earth and erupts from a volcano

mantle the layer of the earth beneath the crust, made of semi-molten rock

pyroclastic flow a scalding avalanche of volcanic gas, dust and rock that rolls down a volcano at speeds of up to 700 kph (450 mph) after an eruption

refugee a person forced to leave his or her home by a natural disaster, war or other event

reservoir a large area of water collected as a water supply for people

satellite an object placed in orbit around the earth in order to provide scientific information

seismic related to movement of the earth and its crust

tectonic plates the massive chunks of crust and mantle that make up the earth's surface

Further Information

FURTHER READING

Eye Witness: Natural Disasters, by Claire Watts (Dorling Kindersley, 2006)

Eye Witness: Volcanoes and Earthquakes, by Susanna Van Rose (Dorling Kindersley, 2004)

Horrible Geography: Earth-Shattering Earthquakes, by Anita Ganeri (Scholastic, 2000)

Shaky Ground: Earthquakes, by Mary Colson (Raintree, 2005)

WEBSITES

National Geographic
www.nationalgeographic.com/forcesofnature

Weather Information
www.weatherwizkids.com/weather-earthquake.htm

History.com
www.history.com/topics/earthquake

Earthquake Facts
www.fema.gov/kids/quake.htm

Index